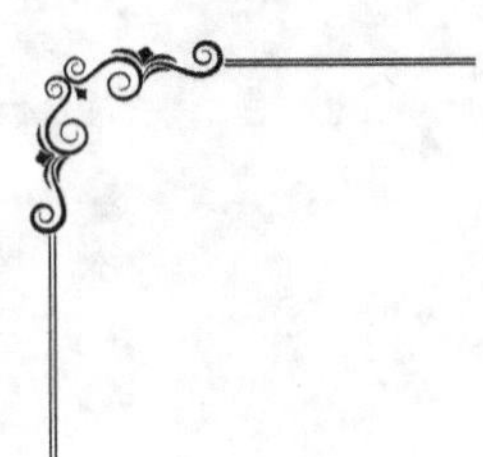

Women

Men

Love

Friendship

Family

Leadership

Money

Society

Life

Happiness

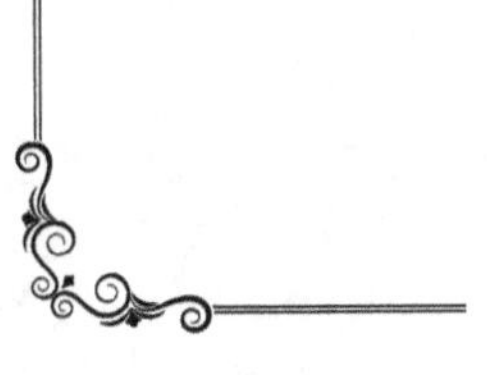

Women

"A woman's guess is much more
accurate than a man's certainty."
- Rudyard Kipling

"A woman is the full circle. Within
her is the power to create,
nurture, and transform."
- Diane Mariechild

"The thing women have yet to
learn is nobody gives you power.
You just take it."
- Roseanne Barr

"Women are the largest untapped
reservoir of talent in the world."
- Hillary Clinton

"Women hold up half the sky."
- Mao Zedong

"Women are the real architects of society."
- Harriet Beecher Stowe

"The empowered woman is powerful beyond measure and beautiful beyond description."
- Steve Maraboli

"The most courageous act is still to think for yourself. Aloud."
- Coco Chanel

"The best protection any woman can have... is courage."
- Elizabeth Cady Stanton

"A woman with a voice is, by definition, a strong woman."
- Melinda Gates

"Women are made to be loved,
not understood."
- Oscar Wilde

"A charming woman doesn't follow
the crowd; she is herself."
- Loretta Young

"The most beautiful makeup of a
woman is passion. But cosmetics
are easier to buy."
- Yves Saint Laurent

"A girl should be two things:
who and what she wants."
- Coco Chanel

"I am a woman phenomenally.
Phenomenal woman, that's me."
- Maya Angelou

"A woman is like a tea bag - you can't tell how strong she is until you put her in hot water."
- Eleanor Roosevelt

"The question isn't who's going to let me; it's who's going to stop me."
- Ayn Rand

"The strength of a woman is not measured by the impact that all her hardships in life have had on her, but the strength of a woman is measured by the extent of her refusal to allow those hardships to dictate her and who she becomes."
- C. JoyBell C.

"A woman is the companion of
man, gifted with equal
mental capacity."
- Mahatma Gandhi

"I do not wish women to have
power over men;
but over themselves."
- Mary Shelley

"The beauty of a woman is not in
the clothes she wears, the figure
that she carries, or the way she
combs her hair. The beauty of a
woman is seen in her eyes
because that is the doorway to her
heart, the place where love
resides."
- Audrey Hepburn

"The age of a woman doesn't mean
a thing. The best tunes are played
on the oldest fiddles."
- Ralph Waldo Emerson

"The history of all times and of
today especially teaches that
women will be forgotten
if they forget to think about
themselves."
- Louise Otto

"Women, if the soul of the nation is
to be saved, I believe that you
must become its soul."
- Coretta Scott King

Men

"A man is but the product of his
thoughts. What he thinks,
he becomes."
- Mahatma Gandhi

"The real man smiles in trouble,
gathers strength from distress,
and grows brave by reflection."
- Thomas Paine

"The measure of a man is what he
does with power."
- Plato

"A man's worth is no greater
than his ambitions."
- Marcus Aurelius

"A man who has no imagination
has no wings."
- Muhammad Ali

"A gentleman is one who puts
more into the world
than he takes out."
- George Bernard Shaw

"A man is rich in proportion to the
number of things he can afford to
let alone."
- Henry David Thoreau

"The true measure of a man is how
he treats someone who can do him
absolutely no good."
- Samuel Johnson

"Men are not prisoners of fate, but
only prisoners of their own minds."
- Franklin D. Roosevelt

"The superior man is modest in his
speech but exceeds in his actions."
- Confucius

"It takes a great man to be
a good listener."
- Calvin Coolidge

"A man who stands for nothing will
fall for anything."
- Malcolm X

"Man's mind, once stretched by a
new idea, never regains its
original dimensions."
- Oliver Wendell Holmes Jr.

"A man is not old until regrets take
the place of dreams."
- John Barrymore

"A man's true wealth is the good he does in this world." - Muhammad

"A man without ethics is a wild beast loosed upon this world." - Albert Camus

"A man is rich not by what he owns, but by what he can do without." - Immanuel Kant

"A real man loves his wife, and places his family as the most important thing in life. Nothing has brought me more peace and content in life than simply being a good husband and father." - Frank Abagnale

Love

"Love is composed of a single soul
inhabiting two bodies."
- Aristotle

"The best thing to hold onto in life
is each other."
- Audrey Hepburn

"To love and be loved is to feel the
sun from both sides."
- David Viscott

"Love is not only something you
feel, it is something you do."
- David Wilkerson

Love is the master key that opens
the gates of happiness."
- Oliver Wendell Holmes Sr.

"Love is an irresistible desire to be irresistibly desired."
- Robert Frost

"Love is like the wind, you can't see it but you can feel it."
- Nicholas Sparks

"The giving of love is an education in itself."
- Eleanor Roosevelt

"Love is a friendship set to music."
- Joseph Campbell

"Love is the flower you've got to let grow."
- John Lennon

"Love is the only force capable of
transforming an enemy
into a friend."
- Martin Luther King Jr.

"Love recognizes no barriers. It
jumps hurdles, leaps fences,
penetrates walls to arrive at its
destination full of hope."
- Maya Angelou

""The only thing we never get
enough of is love; and the only
thing we never give enough
of is love."
- Henry Miller

"We are most alive
when we're in love."
- John Updike

"Where there is love there is life."
- Mahatma Gandhi

"The way to love anything is to
realize that it may be lost."
- Gilbert K. Chesterton

"Love cures people - both the ones
who give it and the ones who
receive it."
- Karl A. Menninger

"Love is like a friendship caught
on fire."
- Bruce Lee

"The art of love is largely
the art of persistence."
- Albert Ellis

"Love is an act of endless
forgiveness, a tender look which
becomes a habit."
- Peter Ustinov

"The best love is the kind that
awakens the soul and makes us
reach for more,
that plants a fire in our hearts and
brings peace to our minds."
- Nicholas Sparks

"Love is an endless mystery, for it
has nothing else to explain it." -
Rabindranath Tagore

"Love is the greatest
refreshment in life."
- Pablo Picasso

"Love does not dominate;
it cultivates."
- Johann Wolfgang von Goethe

"Love is the beauty of the soul." -
Saint Augustine

"The more one judges,
the less one loves."
- Honoré de Balzac

"Being deeply loved by someone
gives you strength, while loving
someone deeply
gives you courage."
- Lao Tzu

"Love all, trust a few,
do wrong to none."
- William Shakespeare

"Love is the voice under all
silences, the hope which has no
opposite in fear; the strength so
strong mere force is feebleness:
the truth more first than sun,
more last than star."
- E.E. Cummings

"Love is a fruit in season at all times, and within reach of every hand." - Mother Teresa

"The greatest happiness of life is the conviction that we are loved; loved for ourselves, or rather, loved in spite of ourselves."
- Victor Hugo

"Love is when the other person's happiness is more important than your own."
- H. Jackson Brown Jr.

Friendship

"A real friend is one who walks in when the rest of the world walks out."
- Walter Winchell

"A friend is someone who knows all about you and still loves you."
- Elbert Hubbard

"True friendship comes when the silence between two people is comfortable."
- David Tyson Gentry

"Friendship is always a sweet responsibility, never an opportunity." - Khalil Gibran

"The greatest gift of life is friendship, and I have received it."
- Hubert H. Humphrey

"Friendship is the source of the greatest pleasures, and without friends even the most agreeable pursuits become tedious."
- Thomas Aquinas

"Friendship is the hardest thing in the world to explain. It's not something you learn in school. But if you haven't learned the meaning of friendship, you really haven't learned anything."
- Muhammad Ali

"Friendship is born at that moment when one person says to another, 'What! You too? I thought I was the only one.'"
- C.S. Lewis

"A true friend is someone who is there for you when he'd rather be anywhere else."
- Len Wein

"A friend is someone who gives you total freedom to be yourself."
- Jim Morrison

"A friend is one who believes in you when you have ceased to believe in yourself."
- Lyman Abbott

"A friend is someone who knows the song in your heart and can sing it back to you when you have forgotten the words."
- C.S. Lewis

"Friendship is the golden thread that ties the heart of all the world."
- John Evelyn

"Friendship marks a life even more deeply than love. Love risks degenerating into obsession, friendship is never anything but sharing." - Elie Wiesel

"Friendship is the inexpressible comfort of feeling safe with a person, having neither to weigh thoughts nor measure words."
- George Eliot

"A friend is one that knows you as you are, understands where you have been, accepts what you have become, and still, gently allows you to grow." - William Shakespeare

Family

"The love of family and the
admiration of friends is much
more important than wealth and
privilege."
- Charles Kuralt

"Family is the compass that
guides us."
- Brad Henry

"Family is not an important thing.
It's everything." -
Michael J. Fox

"Other things may change us, but
we start and end with the family."
- Anthony Brandt

"The family is one of nature's
masterpieces."
- George Santayana

"The family is the first essential
cell of human society."
- Pope John XXIII

"Family means no one gets left
behind or forgotten."
- David Ogden Stiers

"The most important thing in the
world is family and love."
- John Wooden

"Rejoice with your family in the
beautiful land of life!"
- Albert Einstein

"In family life, love is the oil that eases friction, the cement that binds closer together, and the music that brings harmony."
- Friedrich Nietzsche

"The informality of family life is a blessed condition that allows us all to become our best while looking our worst."
- Marge Kennedy

"The bond that links your true family is not one of blood, but of respect and joy in each other's life."
- Richard Bach

"Family is a life jacket in the
stormy sea of life."
- J.K. Rowling

"The strength of a family, like the
strength of an army, lies in its
loyalty to each other."
- Mario Puzo

Leadership

"Leadership is not about being in charge. It's about taking care of those in your charge."
- Simon Sinek

"A genuine leader is not a searcher for consensus but a molder of consensus."
- Martin Luther King Jr.

"The task of the leader is to get their people from where they are to where they have not been."
- Henry Kissinger

"Leadership is the capacity to translate vision into reality."
- Warren Bennis

"Leadership and learning are indispensable to each other."
- John F. Kennedy

"Leadership is the art of getting someone else to do something you want done because
he wants to do it."
- Dwight D. Eisenhower

"The function of leadership is to produce more leaders, not more followers."
- Ralph Nader

"A leader is one who knows the way, goes the way, and shows the way."
- John C. Maxwell

"Leadership is about making others better as a result of your presence and making sure that impact lasts in your absence."
- Sheryl Sandberg

"Leadership is the ability to guide others without force into a direction or decision that leaves them still feeling empowered and accomplished."
- Lisa Cash Hanson

"Leadership is not about being in control. It is about creating conditions for people to fully contribute their unique talents and abilities
towards a common purpose."
- Mike Myatt

"Leadership is solving problems. The day soldiers stop bringing you their problems is the day you have stopped leading them. They have either lost confidence that you can help or concluded you do not care. Either case is a failure of leadership."
- Colin Powell

"The art of leadership is saying no, not saying yes. It is very easy to say yes."
- Tony Blair

"Leadership is not about titles, positions, or flowcharts. It is about one life influencing another."
- John C. Maxwell

"A leader takes people where they
want to go. A great leader takes
people where they don't
necessarily want to go,
but ought to be."
- Rosalynn Carter

"Leadership is influence."
- John C. Maxwell

"The greatest leader is not
necessarily the one who does the
greatest things. He is the one that
gets the people
to do the greatest things."
- Ronald Reagan

"The very essence of leadership is that you have to have a vision. It's got to be a vision you articulate clearly and forcefully on every occasion. You can't blow an uncertain trumpet."
- Rev. Theodore M. Hesburgh

"A leader is best when people barely know he exists. When his work is done, his aim fulfilled, they will say: we did it ourselves."
- Lao Tzu

Money

"Money can't buy happiness, but it will certainly get you a better class of memories."
- Ronald Reagan

"A wise person should have money in their head, but not in their heart."
- Jonathan Swift

"The lack of money is the root of all evil."
- Mark Twain

"Money often costs too much."
- Ralph Waldo Emerson

"Money is a terrible master but an excellent servant."
- P.T. Barnum

"The more you learn,
the more you earn."
- Warren Buffett

"Money is only a tool. It will take
you wherever you wish, but it will
not replace you as the driver."
- Ayn Rand

"Money is a guarantee that we may
have what we want in the future.
Though we need nothing at the
moment, it ensures the possibility
of satisfying a new desire when it
arises."
- Aristotle

"Money is a tool to achieve
freedom, not happiness."
- Dave Ramsey

"Money is multiplied in practical
value depending on the number of
W's you control in your life: what
you do, when you do it, where you
do it, and with whom you do it."
- Timothy Ferriss

"A bank is a place where they lend
you an umbrella in fair weather
and ask for it back when
it starts to rain."
- Robert Frost

"Don't tell me where your priorities
are. Show me where you spend
your money and I'll tell you what
they are."
- James W. Frick

"The greatest reward in becoming a millionaire is not the amount of money that you earn. It is the kind of person that you have to become to become a millionaire in the first place."
- Jim Rohn

"Money can buy you a fine dog, but only love can make it wag its tail."
- Richard Friedman

"It's good to have money and the things that money can buy, but it's good, too, to check up once in a while and make sure that you haven't lost the things that money can't buy."
- George Lorimer

"The lack of money is no obstacle.
The lack of an idea is an obstacle."
- Ken Hakuta

"Money won't create success, the
freedom to make it will."
- Nelson Mandela

"Formal education will make you a
living; self-education will make
you a fortune."
- Jim Rohn

"A simple fact that is hard to learn
is that the time to save money is
when you have some." - Joe Moore
"Never spend your money before
you have it."
- Thomas Jefferson

"Empty pockets never held anyone back. Only empty heads and empty hearts can do that."
- Norman Vincent Peale

"The only way not to think about money is to have a great deal of it."
- Edith Wharton

"Opportunity is missed by most people because it is dressed in overalls and looks like work."
- Thomas Edison

Society

"The measure of a civilization is how it treats its weakest members."
- Mahatma Gandhi

"Injustice anywhere is a threat to justice everywhere." - Martin Luther King Jr.

"Society exists only as a mental concept; in the real world there are only individuals."
- Oscar Wilde

"The only way to deal with an unfree world is to become so absolutely free that your very existence is an act of rebellion."
- Albert Camus

"The world is a dangerous place to live; not because of the people who are evil, but because of the people who don't do anything about it."
- Albert Einstein

"The greatest glory in living lies not in never falling, but in rising every time we fall."
- Nelson Mandela

"The greatness of a nation and its moral progress can be judged by the way its animals are treated."
- Mahatma Gandhi

"The way to gain a good reputation is to endeavor to be what you desire to appear."
- Socrates

"A nation's culture resides in the
hearts and in the
soul of its people."
- Mahatma Gandhi

"No one can make you feel inferior
without your consent."
- Eleanor Roosevelt

"The only thing necessary for evil
to triumph is for good men
to do nothing."
- Edmund Burke

"The greatest glory in living lies
not in never falling, but in rising
every time we fall."
- Nelson Mandela

"The roots of all goodness lie in the
soil of appreciation for goodness."
- Dalai Lama

"To be yourself in a world that is
constantly trying to make you
something else is the greatest
accomplishment."
- Ralph Waldo Emerson

"We may have all come on
different ships, but we're in the
same boat now."
- Martin Luther King Jr.

"You must be the change you wish
to see in the world."
- Mahatma Gandhi

"The world is changed by your
example, not your opinion."
- Paulo Coelho

"In a gentle way, you can shake the
world."
- Mahatma Gandhi

"If you want to lift yourself up,
lift up someone else."
- Booker T. Washington

"The only limit to our realization of
tomorrow will be our
doubts of today."
- Franklin D. Roosevelt

"The future depends on what we
do in the present."
- Mahatma Gandhi

"The world is full of good people, if
you can't find one, be one."
- Mother Teresa

"We make a living by what we get,
but we make a life
by what we give."
- Winston Churchill

"You must not lose faith in
humanity. Humanity is an ocean; if
a few drops of the ocean are dirty,
the ocean does not become dirty."
- Mahatma Gandhi

Life

"Life is a flower of which love is
the honey."
- Victor Hugo

"Life is like a mirror. Smile at it,
and it smiles back at you."
- Peace Pilgrim

"Life is a journey,
not a destination."
- Ralph Waldo Emerson

"Life is not about waiting for the
storms to pass but learning to
dance in the rain."
- Vivian Greene

"Life is a journey that must be
traveled no matter how bad the
roads and accommodations."
- Oliver Goldsmith

"Life is 10% what happens to us
and 90% how we react to it."
- Charles R. Swindoll

"Life is short, and it's up to you to
make it sweet."
- Sarah Louise Delany

"Life is not a problem to be solved,
but a reality to be experienced."
- Soren Kierkegaard

"Life is what we make it, always
has been, always will be."
- Grandma Moses

"Life is about making an impact,
not making an income."
- Kevin Kruse

"Life is like riding a bicycle. To
keep your balance,
you must keep moving."
- Albert Einstein

"Life is like a coin. You can spend
it any way you wish, but
you only spend it once."
- Lillian Dickson

"Life is a succession of lessons
which must be lived
to be understood."
- Helen Keller

"Life is not measured by the
number of breaths we take, but by
the moments that
take our breath away."
- Maya Angelou

"Life is what happens when you're busy making other plans."
- John Lennon

"Life is really simple, but we insist on making it complicated."
- Confucius

"The only impossible journey is the one you never begin."
- Tony Robbins

"Life is either a daring adventure or nothing at all." - Helen Keller
"The biggest adventure you can take is to live the life of your dreams."
- Oprah Winfrey

Happiness

"Happiness is not something ready
made. It comes from
your own actions."
- Dalai Lama

"The best way to cheer yourself
up is to try to cheer
somebody else up."
- Mark Twain

"Happiness depends
upon ourselves."
- Aristotle

"Happiness is not a goal;
it is a by-product."
- Eleanor Roosevelt

"The only joy in the world is
to begin."
- Cesare Pavese

"Happiness is when what you
think, what you say, and what you
do are in harmony."
- Mahatma Gandhi

"The purpose of our lives
is to be happy."
- Dalai Lama

"Happiness is not something you
postpone for the future;
it is something you design
for the present."
- Jim Rohn

"The secret of happiness is not in
doing what one likes, but in liking
what one does."
- J.M. Barrie

"Happiness is not the absence of
problems, it's the ability
to deal with them."
- Steve Maraboli

"The most important thing is to
enjoy your life - to be happy - it's
all that matters."
- Audrey Hepburn

"Happiness is a state of mind. It's
just according to the way
you look at things."
- Walt Disney

"Happiness is when what you
think, what you say, and what you
do are in harmony."
- Mahatma Gandhi

"Happiness is a choice. You can choose to be happy.
There's going to be stress in life, but it's your choice whether you let it affect you or not."
- Valerie Bertinelli

"The only thing that will make you happy is being happy with who you are, and not who people think you are."
- Goldie Hawn

"The only way to find true happiness is to risk being completely cut open."
- Chuck Palahniuk

"The secret of happiness, you see,
is not found in seeking more, but
in developing the capacity
to enjoy less."
- Socrates

"The grand essentials of
happiness are: something to do,
something to love,
and something to hope for."
- Allan K. Chalmers

"The greatest happiness you can
have is knowing that you do not
necessarily require happiness."
- William Saroyan

"Count your age by friends, not
years. Count your life by smiles,
not tears."
- John Lennon

"The foolish man seeks happiness
in the distance; the wise grows it
under his feet."
- James Oppenheim

"Success is not the key to
happiness. Happiness is the key to
success. If you love what you are
doing, you will be successful."
- Albert Schweitzer

"Happiness is not something you
acquire; it's something you are and
something you share."
- John Lennon

"The happiness of your life
depends upon the quality of your
thoughts."
- Marcus Aurelius